D0264244

BY HEART

BY HEART

A Lifetime Companion

*Selected and Edited
by John Bowden*

SCM PRESS LTD

334 00142 0

First published 1984
by SCM Press Ltd
26–30 Tottenham Road London N1

Photoset by The Spartan Press Ltd
Lymington, Hants
and printed in Great Britain by
Richard Clay (The Chaucer Press) Ltd
Bungay, Suffolk

CONTENTS

PREFACE

I never expected to find myself editing what is essentially a collection of prayers, and I doubt whether any of my friends and those who know me well did, either. I have never written anything about prayer, and do not otherwise intend to. But in the wake of all the liturgical changes of the past decade and the proliferation of books of prayers, especially contemporary prayers, one thing has come home to me increasingly strongly: the superficiality and transience of so much of what has been done. Of course there is much to be said for what has happened; but for all its possible benefits it has brought one great loss.

The new words have not grown with us, and there has now been such a flood of them, so often undistinguished, that it is unlikely that they will have the chance, even with the passage of time. They are disposable, and after a while are in fact disposed of, to be replaced with yet newer ones.

We do not react in this way to poetry or other great works of literature. Certainly new works constantly appear, for better or worse, but Donne and Shakespeare, Milton and Hopkins, for example, are not rewritten in modern English because they use archaic forms of expression or words which need a dictionary to explain them. We learn poetry, as we learn music, precisely because it remains the same, and remaining the same actually grows on us over the years, when we get to know it more deeply and it also comes to take on profoundly personal associations. As we say, it becomes part of us.

I believe that prayer is a similar activity. We may be good at putting personal penitence into words, when circumstances force prayer on us, but we are not naturally good at praise and adoration; for those we need a better vocabulary than most of us can usually muster – and that means going back to the long Christian tradition.

At school I was urged to learn as much as possible by heart. There was the prospect of the tedium of military service, with long hours of waiting, doing nothing, and no possibility of passing them with reading, music or natural beauty. I learnt, and the advice stood me in good stead. Then, much later, I had an illustration of its value in a very different context. I was taking Sunday services in an old people's home where the majority had bad eyesight or were hard of hearing. To begin with, it seemed desperately difficult to get through to the group at all. And then I thought of the General Confession and General Thanksgiving from the Book of Common Prayer. As they caught the drift of the words which went far back into their childhood, more and more people joined in, and for a few moments everyone was together, focussed on God.

None of us is likely to escape boredom, fear, illness, forced inactivity, depression, impairment of the senses – and ultimately there will be the approach of death. This collection of prayers, hymns, poetry and prose from the Old Testament to the present day has been made against that background. All of it seems to me to be worth learning by heart – the sooner the better. There is nothing abstruse or out of the way here. I have not had to dig deeply for it or raid anthologies: often I have gone back to a text only to verify wording and punctuation against my fallible memory. All of it is very much part of me; and it is quite deliberately personal.

I offer it as what seems to me the heart of the Christian tradition. As I look at it, all between the same covers, two things in particular strike me. First, the vividness of the imagery and the way in which at times just a single phrase can delight and satisfy the mind – and even after long familiarity and use, everything seems to come up fresh-minted and new. And secondly, the complexity of even the simplest prayers, hymns and poems. Quite unrelated passages are bound together by threads from the wider tapestry of the Christian tradition, and one piece will cast quite unexpected light on another. Teasing out all the connections and implications would be a course in theology by itself.

But intellectual stimulus is not the real purpose of what you will find here. Other religions than Christianity know the power of words repeated, over and over again, until they shape the mind deep into the unconscious. Here are some such words for a lifetime – in the hope of more to come.

Easter 1984   John Bowden

Psalms

*The texts are taken from the translation of the Psalter made by
Miles Coverdale in 1535 and included in the Book of
Common Prayer. Comparison with modern versions based on the
biblical Hebrew in the light of modern scholarship would show
great differences in wording – Coverdale is often inaccurate –
but the Psalms in this version are a devotional work
in their own right.*

This selection ends with two 'canticles': the Te Deum
*is an ancient Christian hymn, traditionally, but improbably,
attributed to St Augustine and St Ambrose; the* Nunc Dimittis,
*from the beginning of the Gospel according to St Luke,
has all the characteristics of an Old Testament psalm,
as was the author's intention.*

God is our hope and strength: a very present help
   in trouble.
Therefore will we not fear, though the earth be moved: and
   though the hills be carried into the midst of the sea.
Though the waters thereof rage and swell: and though the
   mountains shake at the tempest of the same.
The rivers of the flood thereof shall make glad the city of
   God: the holy place of the tabernacle of the most Highest.
God is in the midst of her, therefore shall she not be
   removed: God shall help her, and that right early.
The heathen make much ado, and the kingdoms are moved:
   but God has shewed his voice, and the earth shall
   melt away.
The Lord of hosts is with us: the God of Jacob is our refuge.
O come hither, and behold the works of the Lord: what
   destruction he hath brought upon the earth.
He maketh wars to cease in all the world: he breaketh the
   bow, and knappeth the spear in sunder, and burneth the
   chariots in the fire.
Be still then, and know that I am God: I will be exalted
   among the heathen, and I will be exalted in the earth.
The Lord of hosts is with us: the God of Jacob is our refuge.

Psalm 46

Thou, O God, art praised in Sion: and unto thee shall the
vow be performed in Jerusalem.

Thou that hearest the prayer: unto thee shall all flesh
come.

My misdeeds prevail against me: O be thou merciful unto
our sins.

Blessed is the man, whom thou choosest, and receivest unto
thee: he shall dwell in thy court, and shall be satisfied
with the pleasures of thy house, even of thy holy temple.

Thou shalt shew us wonderful things in thy righteousness,
O God of our salvation: thou that art the hope of all the
ends of the earth, and of them that remain in the
broad sea.

Who in his strength setteth fast the mountains: and is
girded about with power.

Who stilleth the raging of the sea: and the noise of his
waves, and the madness of the people.

They also that dwell in the uttermost parts of the earth shall
be afraid at thy tokens: thou that makest the outgoings of
the morning and evening to praise thee.

Thou visitest the earth and blessest it: thou makest it very
plenteous.

The river of God is full of water: thou preparest their corn,
for so thou providest for the earth.

Thou waterest her furrows, thou sendest rain into the little
valleys thereof: thou makest it soft with the drops of rain,
and blessest the increase of it.

Thou crownest the year with thy goodness: and thy clouds
drop fatness.

They shall drop upon the dwellings of the wilderness:
    and the little hills shall rejoice on every side.
The folds shall be full of sheep: the valleys also shall stand
    so thick with corn, that they shall laugh and sing.

Psalm 65

God be merciful unto us, and bless us: and shew us the light
of his countenance, and be merciful unto us.
That thy way may be known upon earth: thy saving health
among all nations.
Let the people praise thee, O God; yea, let all the people
praise thee.
O let the nations rejoice and be glad: for thou shalt judge the
folk righteously, and govern the nations upon earth.
Let the people praise thee, O God: let all the people
praise thee.
Then shall the earth bring forth her increase: and God,
even our own God, shall give us his blessing.
God shall bless us: and all the ends of the world shall
fear him.

Psalm 67

O how amiable are thy dwellings: thou Lord of hosts!

My soul hath a desire and longing to enter into the courts of
the Lord: my heart and my flesh rejoice in the living God.

Yea, the sparrow hath found her an house, and the swallow
a nest where she may lay her young: even thy altars,
O Lord of hosts, my King and my God.

Blessed are they that dwell in thy house: they will be alway
praising thee.

Blessed is the man whose strength is in thee: in whose heart
are thy ways.

Who going through the vale of misery use it for a well: and
the pools are filled with water.

They will go from strength to strength: and unto the God of
gods appeareth every one of them in Sion.

O Lord God of hosts, hear my prayer: hearken, O God of
Jacob.

Behold, O God our defender: and look upon the face of
thine Anointed.

For one day in thy courts: is better than a thousand.

I had rather be a door-keeper in the house of my God: than
to dwell in the tents of ungodliness.

For the Lord God is a light and defence: the Lord will give
grace and worship, and no good thing shall he withhold
from them that live a godly life.

O Lord God of hosts: blessed is the man that putteth his
trust in thee.

Psalm 84

Lord, thou hast been our refuge: from one generation to
   another.
Before even the mountains were brought forth, or ever the
   earth and the world were made: thou art God from
   everlasting, and world without end.
Thou turnest man to destruction: again thou sayest, Come
   again, ye children of men.
For a thousand years in thy sight are but as yesterday:
   seeing that is past as a watch in the night.
As soon as thou scatterest them they are even as a sleep: and
   fade away suddenly like the grass.
In the morning it is green, and groweth up: but in the
   evening it is cut down, dried up, and withered.
For we consume away in thy displeasure: and are afraid
   at thy wrathful indignation.
Thou hast set our misdeeds before thee: and our secret sins
   in the light of thy countenance.
For when thou art angry all our days are gone: we bring our
   years to an end, as it were a tale that is told.
The days of our age are threescore years and ten; and
   though men be so strong that they come to fourscore
   years: yet is their strength then but labour and sorrow;
   so soon passeth it away, and we are gone.
But who regardeth the power of thy wrath: for even
   thereafter as a man feareth, so is thy displeasure.
So teach us to number our days: that we may apply our
   hearts unto wisdom.
Turn thee again, O Lord, at the last: and be gracious unto
   they servants.

O satisfy us with thy mercy, and that soon: so shall we
     rejoice and be glad all the days of our life.
Comfort us again now after the time that thou hast plagued
     us: and for the years wherein we have suffered adversity.
Shew thy servants thy work and their children thy glory.
And the glorious Majesty of the Lord our God be upon us:
     prosper thou the work of our hands upon us,
     O prosper thou our handy-work.

Psalm 90

Whoso dwelleth under the defence of the most High: shall
abide under the shadow of the Almighty.

I will say unto the Lord, Thou art my hope, and my strong
hold: my God, in him will I trust.

For he shall deliver thee from the snare of the hunter; and
from the noisome pestilence.

He shall defend thee under his wings, and thou shalt be safe
under his feathers: his faithfulness and truth shall be thy
shield and buckler.

Thou shalt not be afraid for any terror by night: nor for the
arrow that flyeth by day;

For the pestilence that walketh in darkness: nor for the
sickness that destroyeth in the noon-day.

A thousand shall fall beside thee, and ten thousand at thy
right hand: but it shall not come nigh thee.

Yea, with thine eyes shalt thou behold: and see the reward
of the ungodly.

For thou, Lord, art my hope: thou hast set thine house of
defence very high.

There shall no evil happen unto thee: neither shall any
plague come nigh thy dwelling.

For he shall give his angels charge over thee: to keep thee
in all thy ways.

They shall bear thee in their hands: that thou hurt not thy
foot against a stone.

Thou shalt go upon the lion and adder: the young lion and
the dragon shalt thou tread under thy feet.

Because he hath set his love upon me, therefore will I deliver
him: I will set him up, because he hath known my name.

He shall call upon me, and I will hear him: yea, I am
    with him in trouble; I will deliver him, and bring him
    to honour.
With long life will I satisfy him: and show him my salvation.

Psalm 91

Lord, thou art become gracious unto thy land: thou hast
   turned away the captivity of Jacob.
Thou hast forgiven the offence of thy people: and covered
   all their sins.
Thou hast taken away all thy displeasure: and turned
   thyself from thy wrathful indignation.
Turn us then, O God our Saviour: and let thine anger
   cease from us.
Wilt thou not turn again, and quicken us: that thy people
   may rejoice in thee?
Shew us thy mercy, O Lord: and grant us thy salvation.
I will hearken what the Lord God will say concerning me:
   for he shall speak peace unto his people, and to his saints,
   that they turn not again.
For his salvation is nigh them that fear him: that glory may
   dwell in our land,
Mercy and truth are met together: righteousness and peace
   have kissed each other.
Truth shall flourish out of the earth: and righteousness hath
   looked down from heaven.
Yea, the Lord shall show loving-kindness: and our land
   shall give her increase.
Righteousness shall go before him: and he shall direct his
   going in the way.

Psalm 85

The Lord is King, and hath put on glorious apparel: the Lord
   hath put on his apparel, and girded himself with
   strength.
He hath made the round world so sure: that it cannot be
   moved.
Ever since the world began hath thy seat been prepared:
   thou art from everlasting.
The floods are risen, O Lord, the floods have lift up their
   voice: the floods lift up their waves.
The waves of the sea are mighty, and rage horribly: but yet
   the Lord, who dwelleth on high, is mightier.
Thy testimonies, O Lord, are very sure: holiness becometh
   thine house for ever.

Psalm 93

O sing unto the Lord a new song: for he hath done
    marvellous things.
With his own right hand, and with his holy arm: hath he
    gotten himself the victory.
The Lord declared his salvation: his righteousness hath he
    openly shewed in the sight of the heathen.
He hath remembered his mercy and truth toward the house
    of Israel: and all the ends of the world have seen the
    salvation of our God.
Shew yourselves joyful unto the Lord, all ye lands: sing,
    rejoice and give thanks.
Praise the Lord upon the harp: sing to the harp with a psalm
    of thanksgiving.
With trumpets also, and shawms: O shew yourselves joyful
    before the Lord the King.
Let the sea make a noise, and all that therein is: the round
    world, and they that dwell therein.
Let the floods clap their hands, and let the hills be joyful
    together before the Lord: for he is come to judge the
    earth.
With righteousness shall he judge the world: and the people
    with equity.

Psalm 98

O be joyful in the Lord, all ye lands: serve the Lord with
    gladness, and come before his presence with a song.
Be ye sure that the Lord he is God: it is he that hath made us,
    and not we ourselves; we are his people, and the sheep of
    his pasture.
O go your way into his gates with thanksgiving, and into his
    courts with praise: be thankful unto him, and speak good
    of his name.
For the Lord is gracious, his mercy is everlasting: and his
    truth endureth from generation to generation.

Psalm 100

Thou, Lord, in the beginning hast laid the foundations of
the earth: and the heavens are the work of thy hands.
They shall perish, but thou shalt endure: they all shall wax
old as doth a garment;
And as a vesture shalt thou change them, and they shall be
changed: but thou art the same, and thy years shall not
fail.
The children of thy servants shall continue: and their seed
shall stand fast in thy sight.

From Psalm 102

The Lord is full of compassion and mercy: long-suffering, and of great goodness.

He will not alway be chiding: neither keepeth he his anger for ever.

He hath not dealt with us after our sins: nor rewarded us according to our wickednesses.

For look how high the heaven is in comparison of the earth: so great is his mercy also toward them that fear him.

Look how wide also the east is from the west; so far hath he set our sins from us.

Yea, like as a father pitieth his own children: even so is the Lord merciful unto them that fear him.

For he knoweth whereof we are made: he remembereth that we are but dust.

The days of man are but as grass: for he flourisheth as a flower of the field.

For as soon as the wind goeth over it, it is gone: and the place thereof shall know it no more.

But the merciful goodness of the Lord endureth for ever and ever upon them that fear him: and his righteousness upon children's children.

Even upon such as keep his covenant: and think upon his commandments to do them.

From Psalm 103

I will lift up mine eyes unto the hills: from whence cometh
  my help.
My help cometh even from the Lord: who hath made
  heaven and earth.
He will not suffer thy foot to be moved: and he that keepeth
  thee will not sleep.
Behold, he that keepeth Israel: shall neither slumber nor
  sleep.
The Lord himself is thy keeper: the Lord is thy defence upon
  thy right hand;
So that the sun shall not burn thee by day: neither the moon
  by night.
The Lord shall preserve thee from all evil: yea, it is even he
  that shall keep thy soul.
The Lord shall preserve thy going out, and thy coming in:
  from this time forth for evermore.

Psalm 121

Out of the deep have I called unto thee, O Lord: Lord, hear
   my voice.
O let thine ears consider well: the voice of my complaint.
If thou, Lord, wilt be extreme to mark what is done amiss:
   O Lord, who may abide it?
For there is mercy with thee: therefore shalt thou be feared.
I look for the Lord; my soul doth wait for him: in his word is
   my trust.
My soul fleeth unto the Lord: before the morning watch,
   I say, before the morning watch.
O Israel, trust in the Lord, for with the Lord there is mercy:
   and with him is plenteous redemption.
And he shall redeem Israel: from all his sins.

Psalm 130

O Lord, thou hast searched me out, and known me:
   thou knowest my down-sitting, and mine up-rising;
   thou understandest my thoughts long before.
Thou art about my path, and about my bed: and spiest out
   all my ways.
For lo, there is not a word in my tongue: but thou, O Lord,
   knowest it altogether.
Thou hast fashioned me behind and before: and laid thine
   hand upon me.
Such knowledge is too wonderful and excellent for me:
   I cannot attain unto it.
Whither shall I go then from thy Spirit: or whither shall I go
   then from thy presence?
If I climb up into heaven, thou art there: if I go down to hell,
   thou art there also.
If I take the wings of the morning: and remain in the
   uttermost parts of the sea;
Even there also shall thy hand lead me: and thy right hand
   shall hold me.
If I say, Peradventure the darkness shall cover me: then
   shall my night be turned to day.
Yea, the darkness is no darkness with thee, but the light is
   as clear as the day: the darkness and light to thee are
   both alike.
For my reins are thine: thou hast covered me in my mother's
   womb.
I will give thanks unto thee, for I am fearfully and
   wonderfully made: marvellous are thy works, and that
   my soul knoweth right well.

My bones are not hid from thee: though I be made secretly,
   and fashioned beneath in the earth.
Thine eyes did see my substance, yet being unperfect: and
   in thy book were all my members written;
Which day by day were fashioned: when as yet there was
   none of them.
How dear are thy counsels unto me, O God: O how great is
   the sum of them!
If I tell them, they are more in number than the sand:
   when I wake up, I am present with thee.

From Psalm 139

Behold now, praise the Lord: all ye servants of the Lord;
Ye that by night stand in the house of the Lord: even in the
   courts of the house of our God.
Lift up your hands in the sanctuary: and praise the Lord.
The Lord that made heaven and earth: give thee blessing
   out of Sion.

Psalm 134

Praise the Lord, O my soul; while I live will I praise the Lord:
yea, as long as I have any being, I will sing praises unto
my God.

O put not your trust in princes, nor in any child of man: for
there is no help in them.

For when the breath of man goeth forth he shall turn again
to his earth: and then all his thoughts perish.

Blessed is he that hath the God of Jacob for his help: and
whose hope is in the Lord his God;

Who made heaven and earth, the sea, and all that therein is:
who keepeth his promise for ever;

Who helpeth them to right that suffer wrong: who feedeth
the hungry.

The Lord looseth men out of prison: the Lord giveth sight to
the blind.

The Lord helpeth them that are fallen: the Lord careth for
the righteous.

The Lord careth for the strangers; he defendeth the
fatherless and widow: as for the way of the ungodly,
he turneth it upside down.

The Lord thy God, O Sion, shall be King for evermore: and
throughout all generations.

Psalm 146

O praise the Lord of heaven: praise him in the height.
Praise him, all ye angels of his: praise him, all his host.
Praise him, sun and moon: praise him, all ye stars and light.
Praise him, all ye heavens: and ye waters that are above the
    heavens.
Let them praise the name of the Lord: for he spake the word,
    and they were made; he commanded, and they were
    created.
He hath made them fast for ever and ever: he hath
    given them a law which shall not be broken.
Praise the Lord upon earth: ye dragons, and all deeps;
Fire and hail, snow and vapours: wind and storm, fulfilling
    his word;
Mountains and all hills: fruitful trees and all cedars.
Beasts and all cattle: worms and feathered fowls.
Kings of the earth and all people; princes and all judges
    of the world.
Young men and maidens, old men and children, praise the
    name of the Lord; for his name only is excellent,
    and his praise above heaven and earth.
He shall exalt the horn of his people; all his saints shall
    praise him: even the children of Israel,
    even the people that serveth him.

Psalm 148

O praise God in his holiness: praise him in the firmament of his power.

Praise him in his noble acts: praise him according to his excellent greatness.

Praise him in the sound of the trumpet: praise him upon the lute and harp.

Praise him in the cymbals and dances: praise him upon the strings and pipe.

Praise him upon the well-tuned cymbals: praise him upon the loud cymbals.

Let everything that hath breath: praise the Lord.

Psalm 150

We praise thee, O God: we acknowledge thee
  to be the Lord.
All the earth doth worship thee: the Father everlasting.
To thee all Angels cry aloud: the Heavens and all the Powers
  therein.
To thee Cherubin, and Seraphin: continually do cry,
Holy, Holy, Holy: Lord God of Sabaoth; heaven and earth
  are full of the Majesty: of thy Glory.
The glorious company of the Apostles: praise thee.
The noble army of Martyrs: praise thee.
The holy Church throughout all the world:
  doth acknowledge thee;
The Father: of an infinite Majesty;
Thine honourable, true: and only Son;
Also the Holy Ghost: the Comforter.

Thou art the King of Glory: O Christ.
Thou art the everlasting Son: of the Father.
When thou tookest upon thee to deliver man: thou didst not
  abhor the Virgin's womb.
When thou hadst overcome the sharpness of death: thou
  didst open the Kingdom of Heaven to all believers.
Thou sittest at the right hand of God: in the Glory of the
  Father.
We believe that thou shalt come: to be our Judge.
We therefore pray thee, help thy servants: whom thou hast
  redeemed with thy precious blood.
Make them to be numbered with thy saints: in glory
  everlasting.

O Lord, save thy people: and bless thine heritage.
Govern them: and lift them up for ever.
Day by day: we magnify thee.
And we worship thy name: ever world without end.
Vouchsafe, O Lord: to keep us this day without sin.
O Lord, have mercy upon us: have mercy upon us.
O Lord, let thy mercy lighten upon us: as our trust is in thee.
O Lord, in thee have I trusted: let me never be confounded.

Te Deum

Lord, now lettest thou thy servant depart in peace:
   according to thy word.
For mine eyes have seen: thy salvation.
Which thou hast prepared: before the face of all people.
To be a light to lighten the Gentiles: and to be the glory of
   thy people Israel.

Glory be to the Father, and to the Son: and to the Holy
   Ghost;
As it was in the beginning, is now, and ever shall be:
   world without end. Amen.

Nunc Dimittis

Collects

From the Book of Common Prayer

'Collect' is an old term, denoting the collection of the petitions of the congregation into a single prayer. Many of the collects in the Book of Common Prayer are translations from the mediaeval Latin, while others were Archbishop Cranmer's own work. Although most are associated in the Prayer Book with specific Sundays, those included here can be said at any time.

O God, who knowest us to be set in the midst of so many and great dangers, that by reason of the frailty of our nature we cannot always stand upright; Grant to us such strength and protection, as may support us in all dangers, and carry us through all temptations; through Jesus Christ our Lord.

Epiphany IV

Almighty God, who seest that we have no power of ourselves to help ourselves; Keep us both outwardly in our bodies, and inwardly in our souls; that we may be defended from all adversities which may happen to the body, and from all evil thoughts which may assault and hurt the soul; through Jesus Christ our Lord.

Lent II

Almighty and everlasting God, who, of thy tender love towards mankind, hast sent thy Son our Saviour Jesus Christ, to take upon him our flesh, and to suffer death upon the cross, that all mankind should follow the example of his great humility; Mercifully grant, that we may both follow the example of his patience, and also be made partakers of his resurrection, through the same Jesus Christ our Lord.

Palm Sunday

Almighty God, we beseech thee graciously to behold this thy family, for which our Lord Jesus Christ was contented to be betrayed, and given up into the hands of wicked men, and to suffer death upon the cross, who now liveth and reigneth with thee and the Holy Ghost, ever one God, world without end.

Good Friday

O God, the protector of all that trust in thee, without whom nothing is strong, nothing is holy; Increase and multiply upon us thy mercy; that, thou being our ruler and guide, we may so pass through things temporal that we finally lose not the things eternal: Grant this, O heavenly Father, for Jesus Christ's sake our Lord.

Trinity IV

O God, who hast prepared for them that love thee such good things as pass man's understanding: Pour into our hearts such love toward thee, that we, loving thee above all things, may obtain thy promises, which exceed all that we can desire, through Jesus Christ our Lord.

Trinity VI

Lord of all power and might, who art the author and giver of all good things: Graft in our hearts the love of thy Name, increase in us true religion, nourish us with all goodness, and of thy great mercy keep us in the same; through Jesus Christ our Lord.

Trinity VII

O God, who declarest thy almighty power most chiefly in shewing mercy and pity: Mercifully grant unto us such a measure of thy grace, that we, running the way of thy commandments, may obtain thy gracious promises, and be made partakers of thy heavenly treasure; through Jesus Christ our Lord.

Trinity XI

Almighty and everlasting God, who art always more ready to hear than we to pray, and art wont to give more than either we desire, or deserve; Pour down upon us the abundance of thy mercy; forgiving us those things whereof our conscience is afraid, and giving us those good things which we are not worthy to ask, but through the merits and mediation of Jesus Christ, thy Son our Lord.

Trinity XII

Almighty and everlasting God, give unto us the increase of faith, hope and charity; and, that we may obtain that which thou dost promise, make us to love that which thou dost command; through Jesus Christ our Lord.

Trinity XIV

O Almighty and most merciful God, of thy bountiful
goodness keep us, we beseech thee, from all things that
may hurt us; that we, being ready both in body and soul,
may cheerfully accomplish those things that thou
wouldest have done; through Jesus Christ our Lord.

Trinity XX

O God, who art the author of peace and lover of concord,
in knowledge of whom standeth our eternal life, whose
service is perfect freedom; Defend us thy humble servants
in all assaults of our enemies; that we, surely
trusting in thy defence, may not fear the power of any
adversaries, through the might of Jesus Christ our Lord.

Morning Prayer

O Lord, our heavenly Father, Almighty and everlasting God, who hast safely brought us to the beginning of this day: Defend us in the same with thy mighty power; and grant that this day we fall into no sin, neither run into any kind of danger, but that all our doings may be ordered by thy governance, to do all that is righteous in thy sight; through Jesus Christ our Lord.

Morning Prayer

O God, from whom all holy desires, all good counsels and all just works do proceed; Give unto thy servants that peace which the world cannot give; that both our hearts may be set to obey thy commandments, and also that by thee, we being defended from the fear of our enemies may pass our time in rest and quietness; through the merits of Jesus Christ our Saviour.

Evening Prayer

Lighten our darkness, we beseech thee, O Lord; and by thy great mercy defend us from all perils and dangers of this night; for the love of thy only Son, our Saviour, Jesus Christ.

Evening Prayer

Almighty God, the fountain of all wisdom, who knowest our necessities before we ask, and our ignorance in asking; We beseech thee to have compassion upon our infirmities; and those things, which for our unworthiness we dare not, and for our blindness we cannot ask, vouchsafe to give us, for the worthiness of thy Son Jesus Christ our Lord.

Communion Service

Prayers

*This selection of brief prayers from the Christian tradition,
beginning with the Lord's Prayer, is just a fragment of its riches.
Some of the prayers may be found elsewhere with slightly
different wording; I have not attempted to discover the original
or most authentic form – in some cases that is impossible.
Nor have I tried to trace prayers back to their earliest source;
as with the collects, some of them first appeared well before the
prayer book from which they are usually quoted.
Some prayers are anonymous; others have the names of
individual authors against them, but it should be remembered that
all the prayers ultimately go back to individuals.
Like other great works of art, they are not produced by committees.
The prayers in this section follow an approximate
chronological order.*

Our Father, which art in heaven,
Hallowed be thy name;
Thy kingdom come;
Thy will be done;
In earth as it is in heaven.
Give us this day our daily bread.
And forgive us our trespasses,
As we forgive them that trespass against us.
And lead us not into temptation;
But deliver us from evil.
For thine is the kingdom,
The power, and the glory,
For ever and ever.
Amen.

The Lord's Prayer as in the Book of Common Prayer

Into thy hands, O Lord, we commend our spirits, souls, and bodies, for thou hast created and redeemed them, O Lord God Almighty. Guide us and all whom we love this day, and kindle thy light in our hearts, that thy godly knowledge increasing in us more and more, we may always be found to walk and live after thy will and pleasure; through Jesus Christ our Lord.

Ancient Collect

Be present, O merciful God, and protect us through the silent hours of this night, so that we who are wearied by the changes and chances of this fleeting world may rest upon thine eternal changelessness; through the everlasting Christ our Lord.

Ancient Collect

O Lord, our Saviour, who hast warned us that thou wilt
require much of those to whom much is given: grant that
we whose lot is cast in so goodly a heritage may strive
together more abundantly by prayer and by every other
means to extend to others what we so richly enjoy, that as
we have entered into the labours of others, we may so
labour that others may enter into ours, to the fulfilment of
thy holy will, and the salvation of all mankind.

Fourth century

Almighty God, in whom we live and move and have our
being, who hast made us for thyself, so that our hearts are
restless till they rest in thee: Grant us purity of heart and
strength of purpose, that no selfish passion may hinder
us from knowing thy will, no weakness from doing it;
but that in thy light we may see light clearly, and in thy
service find our perfect freedom; through Jesus Christ
our Lord.

St Augustine

O God, who art the light of the minds that know thee, the life of the souls that love thee, and the strength of the wills that seek thee, help us so to know thee that we may truly love thee, so to love thee that we may fully serve thee, whose service is perfect freedom; through Jesus Christ our Lord.

Gelasian Sacramentary

O God of unchangeable power and eternal light, look favourably on thy whole church, that wonderful and sacred mystery; and by the tranquil operation of thy perpetual providence, carry out the work of man's salvation; and let the whole world feel and see that things which were cast down are being raised up, that those things which had grown old are being made new, and that all things are returning to perfection through him from whom they took their origin, even through our Lord Jesus Christ.

Gelasian Sacramentary

Preserve us, O Lord, while waking, and guard us while sleeping, that awake we may watch with Christ, and asleep we may rest in peace.

Roman Breviary

Thanks be unto thee, our Lord Jesus Christ: for all the benefits which thou hast given us; for all the pains and insults which thou hast borne for us. O most merciful Redeemer, friend and brother: may we know thee more clearly, love thee more dearly, and follow thee more nearly, now and ever.

St Richard of Chichester

Lord, make us the instruments of thy peace;
   Where there is hatred, let us sow love;
   Where there is injury, pardon;
   Where there is doubt, faith;
   Where there is despair, hope;
   Where there is sadness, joy;
   Where there is darkness, light.
Grant that we may not seek so much to be consoled,
   as to console;
   to be understood, as to understand;
   to be loved, as to love;
For in giving we receive, in pardoning we are pardoned,
   and in dying we are born into eternal life.

St Francis of Assisi

Teach us, good Lord, to serve thee as thou deservest;
to give, and not to count the cost; to fight and not to heed
the wounds; to toil and not to seek for rest; to labour and not
to ask for any reward save the joy of knowing that we do
thy will.

Ignatius Loyola

God be in my head,
And in my understanding;
God be in my eyes,
And in my looking;
God be in my mouth,
And in my speaking;
God be in my heart,
And in my thinking;
God be at mine end,
And at my departing.

Fifteenth century

Christ has no body now on earth but yours, no hands but
yours, no feet but yours; yours are the eyes through which
is to look out Christ's compassion to the world, yours are
the feet with which he is to go about doing good, and yours
are the hands with which he is to bless us now.

St Teresa of Avila

O Lord Jesus Christ, who art the way, the truth, and the life:
suffer us not, we pray thee, to stray from thee, who art
the way; nor to distrust thee, who art the truth; nor to rest in
any other thing than thee, who art the life. Teach us by thy
Holy Spirit what to believe, what to do, and wherein to take
our rest. We ask it for thy Name's sake.

Erasmus

Bring us, O Lord God, at our last awakening into the house
and gate of heaven, to enter into that gate and dwell in that
house, where there shall be no darkness nor dazzling, but
one equal light; no noise nor silence, but one equal music;
no fears nor hopes, but one equal possession; no ends nor
beginnings, but one equal eternity; in the habitations of thy
glory and dominion, world without end.

John Donne

Almighty God, Father of all mercies, we thine unworthy
servants do give thee most humble and hearty thanks for all
thy goodness and loving-kindness to us and to all men.
We bless thee for our creation, preservation, and all the
blessings of this life; but above all, for thine inestimable love
in the redemption of the world by our Lord Jesus Christ;
for the means of grace and for the hope of glory. And,
we beseech thee, give us that due sense of all thy mercies,
that our hearts may be unfeignedly thankful, and that we
shew forth thy praise, not only with our lips but in our lives;
by giving up ourselves to thy service, and by walking
before thee in holiness and righteousness all our days;
through Jesus Christ our Lord, to whom with thee and the
Holy Ghost be all honour and glory, world without end.

Book of Common Prayer

O God, the Creator and Preserver of all mankind, we
humbly beseech thee for all sorts and conditions of men;
that thou wouldest be pleased to make thy ways known
unto them, thy saving health unto all nations. More
especially, we pray for the good estate of thy Catholic
Church; that it may be so guided and governed by thy good
Spirit, that all who profess and call themselves Christians
may be led into the way of truth, and hold the faith in unity
of spirit, in the bond of peace, and in righteousness of life.
Finally, we commend to thy fatherly goodness all those,
who are any ways afflicted, or distressed, in mind, body, or
estate; that it may please thee to comfort and relieve them,
according to their several necessities, giving them patience
under their sufferings, and a happy issue out of all their
afflictions. And this we beg for Jesus Christ his sake.

Book of Common Prayer

O God, who hast brought us near to an innumerable
company of angels, and to the spirits of just men made
perfect: Grant us during our pilgrimage to abide in their
fellowship, and in our heavenly country to become
partakers of their joy; through Jesus Christ our Lord.

William Bright

O Thou who makest the stars, and turnest the shadow of
death into the morning, we render thee, our Lord and King,
the tribute of our praise; for the resurrection of the
springtime, for the everlasting hopes that rise within the
human heart, and for the gospel which has brought life and
immortality to light. Receive our thanksgiving, reveal thy
presence, and send forth into our hearts the Spirit of the
risen Christ.

W. E. Orchard

Abide with us, Lord, for it is toward evening and the day is far spent. Abide with us and with thy whole Church. Abide with us in the end of the day, in the end of our life, in the end of the world. Abide with us in thy grace and bounty, with thy holy Word and sacrament, with thy comfort and blessing. Abide with us when comes the night of affliction and fear, the night of doubt and temptation, the night of bitter death. Abide with us and with all thy faithful ones, O Lord, in time and in eternity.

Lutheran Church

O Lord, support us all the day long of this troublous life, until the shades lengthen, and the evening comes, and the busy world is hushed, the fever of life is over, and our work is done. Then, Lord, in thy mercy, grant us safe lodging, a holy rest, and peace at the last, through Jesus Christ our Lord.

1928 Prayer Book

Remember, O Lord, what thou hast wrought in us, and not what we deserve, and as thou hast called us to thy service, make us worthy of our calling; through Jesus Christ our Lord.

1928 Prayer Book

O Lord Jesus Christ, who didst say to thine Apostles, Peace I leave with you, my peace I give unto you: Regard not our sins, but the faith of thy Church, and grant it that peace and unity which is agreeable to thy will; who livest and reignest with the Father and the Holy Spirit, one God, world without end.

1928 Prayer Book

O God, who hast made of one blood all nations of men for to dwell on the face of the earth, and didst send thy blessed Son Jesus Christ to preach peace to them that are afar off, and to them that are nigh: Grant that all the peoples of the world may feel after thee and find thee; and hasten, O Lord, the fulfilment of thy promise, to pour out thy Spirit upon all flesh; through Jesus Christ our Lord.

1928 Prayer Book

Almighty God, from whom all thoughts of truth and peace proceed: Kindle, we pray thee, in the hearts of all men the true love of peace; and guide with thy pure and peaceable wisdom those who take counsel for the nations of the earth; that in tranquillity thy kingdom may go forward, till the earth is filled with the knowledge of thy love; through Jesus Christ our Lord.

1928 Prayer Book

Almighty God, whose blessed Son Jesus Christ went about doing good, and healing all manner of sickness and all manner of disease among the people: Continue, we beseech thee, this his gracious work among us; cheer, heal and sanctify the sick; grant to the physicians, surgeons, and nurses wisdom and skill, sympathy and patience; and send down thy blessing on all who labour to prevent suffering and to forward thy purposes of love; through Jesus Christ our Lord.

1928 Prayer Book

O heavenly Father, who in thy Son Jesus Christ hast given us a true faith, and a sure hope: Help us, we pray thee, to live as those who believe and trust in the Communion of Saints, the forgiveness of sins, and the resurrection to life everlasting, and strengthen this faith and hope in us all the days of our life: through the love of thy Son, Jesus Christ our Saviour.

1928 Prayer Book

Father of all, we give you thanks and praise, that when we were still far off you met us in your Son and brought us home. Dying and living, he declared your love, gave us grace, and opened the gate of glory. May we who share Christ's body live his risen life; we who drink his cup bring life to others; we whom the Spirit lights give light to the world. Keep us firm in the hope you have set before us, so we and all your children shall be free, and the whole earth live to praise your name; through Christ our Lord.

Alternative Service Book 1980

Hymns and Poems

*In our modern world, the word 'hymn' tends to suggest a lower
level of inspiration than 'poem', so I have used both words in
the title. But what you will find here is above all a selection of
fine verse, much of which has been set to music, and which is either
in praise of God or an expression of highest human aspiration.
I have tried deliberately not to make it a collection of
religious poetry.
The sequence runs from morning to evening, and through
Easter to Pentecost.*

Lord, be thy word my rule,
In it may I rejoice;
Thy glory be my aim,
Thy holy will my choice;

Thy promises my hope,
Thy providence my guard,
Thine arm my strong support,
Thyself my great reward.

Bishop Christopher Wordsworth

Forth in thy name, O Lord, I go,
My daily labour to pursue;
Thee, only thee, resolved to know,
In all I think, or speak, or do.

The task thy wisdom hath assigned
O let me cheerfully fulfil;
In all my works thy presence find,
And prove thine acceptable will.

Preserve me from my calling's snare,
And hide my simple heart above,
Above the thorns of choking care,
The gilded baits of worldly love.

Thee may I set at my right hand,
Whose eyes my inmost substance see,
And labour on at thy command,
And offer all my works to thee.

Give me to bear thy easy yoke,
And every moment watch and pray,
And still to things eternal look,
And hasten to thy glorious day;

For thee delightfully employ
Whate'er thy bounteous grace hath given,
And run my course with even joy,
And closely walk with thee to heaven.

Charles Wesley

My God, I love thee; not because
I hope for heaven thereby,
Nor yet because who love thee not
Are lost eternally.

Thou, O my Jesus, thou didst me
Upon the Cross embrace;
For me didst bear the nails and spear;
And manifold disgrace,

And griefs and torments numberless,
And sweat of agony;
E'en death itself; and all for one
Who was thine enemy.

Then why, O blessed Jesu Christ,
Should I not love thee well,
Not for the sake of winning heaven
Or of escaping hell;

Not with the hope of gaining aught,
Not seeking a reward;
But as thyself hast loved me,
O ever-loving Lord!

E'en so I love thee, and will love,
And in thy praise will sing,
Solely because thou art my God,
And my eternal King.

Seventeenth-century Latin,
translated E. Caswall

Alleluya! Alleluya!
Hearts to heaven and voices raise;
Sing to God a hymn of gladness,
Sing to God a hymn of praise;
He who on the Cross a victim
For the world's salvation bled,
Jesus Christ, the King of glory,
Now is risen from the dead.

Christ is risen, Christ the first-fruits
Of the holy harvest field,
Which will all its full abundance
At his second coming yield;
Then the golden ears of harvest
Will their heads before him wave,
Ripened by his glorious sunshine
From the furrows of the grave.

Christ is risen, we are risen;
Shed upon us heavenly grace,
Rain, and dew, and gleams of glory
From the brightness of thy face;
That we, Lord, with hearts in heaven
Here on earth may fruitful be,
And by angel-hands be gathered
And be ever safe with thee.

Alleluya! Alleluya!
Glory be to God on high;
To the Father, and the Saviour;
Who has gained the victory;
Glory to the Holy Spirit,
Fount of love and sanctity;
Alleluya! Alleluya!
To the Triune Majesty.

Bishop Christopher Wordsworth

Rise, heart, Thy Lord is risen; sing His praise
                    Without delayes,
Who takes thee by the hand, that thou likewise
                    With Him mayst rise;
That, as His death calcinèd thee to dust,
His life may make thee gold, and, much more, just.

Awake, my lute, and struggle for thy part
                    With all thy art:
The crosse taught all wood to resound His name
                    Who bore the same;
His stretchèd sinews taught all strings what key
Is best to celebrate this most high day.

Consort both heart and lute, and twist a song
                    Pleasant and long;
Or, since all musick is but three parts vied
                    And multiplied,
O, let Thy blessèd Spirit bear a part,
And make up our defects with His sweet art.

George Herbert

Most glorious Lord of life, that on this day
Didst make thy triumph over death and sin,
And having harrowed hell, didst bring away
Captivity thence captive, us to win:
This joyous day, dear Lord, with joy begin,
And grant that we for whom thou diddest die,
Being with thy dear Blood clean washed from sin,
May live for ever in felicity:
And that thy love we weighing worthily,
May likewise love thee for the same again;
And for thy sake, that all like dear didst buy,
With love may one another entertain;
So let us love, dear Love, like as we ought:
Love is the lesson which the Lord us taught.

Edmund Spenser

Come down, O Love divine,
Seek thou this soul of mine,
And visit it with thine own ardour glowing;
O comforter, draw near,
Within my heart appear;
And kindle it, thy holy flame bestowing.

O let it freely burn,
Till earthly passions turn
To dust and ashes in its heat consuming;
And let thy glorious light
Shine ever on my sight,
And clothe me round, the while my path illuming.

Let holy charity
Mine outward vesture be,
And lowliness become mine inner clothing;
True lowliness of heart,
Which takes the humbler part,
And o'er its own shortcomings weeps with loathing.

Bianco da Siena, translated R. F. Littledale

Come, my Way, my Truth, my Life!
Such a Way as gives us breath,
Such a Truth as ends all strife,
Such a Life as killeth Death.

Come, my Light, my Feast, my Strength!
Such a Light as shows a feast,
Such a Feast as mends in length,
Such a Strength as makes his guest.

Come, my Joy, my Love, my Heart!
Such a Joy as none can move,
Such a Love as none can part,
Such a Heart as joyes in love.

George Herbert

O King enthroned on high,
Thou comforter divine,
Blest Spirit of all truth, be nigh
And make us thine.

Thou art the source of life,
Thou art our treasure store;
Give us thy peace, and end our strife
For evermore.

Descend, O heavenly Dove,
Abide with us alway;
And in the fulness of thy love
Cleanse us, we pray.

Pentecostarion, translated J. Brownlie

O Thou who camest from above,
The pure celestial fire to impart,
Kindle a flame of sacred love
On the mean altar of my heart.

There let it for thy glory burn
With inextinguishable blaze,
And trembling to its source return
In humble prayer, and fervent praise.

Jesus, confirm my heart's desire
To work, and speak, and think for thee;
Still let me guard the holy fire,
And still stir up thy gift in me.

Ready for all thy perfect will,
My acts of faith and love repeat,
Till death thy endless mercies seal,
And make my sacrifice complete.

Charles Wesley

Tell out, my soul, the greatness of the Lord:
unnumbered blessings, give my spirit voice;
Tender to me the promise of his word;
in God my Saviour shall my heart rejoice.

Tell out my soul, the greatness of his name;
make known his might, the deeds his arm has done;
His mercy sure, from age to age the same;
his holy name, the Lord, the Mighty One.

Tell out, my soul, the greatness of his might:
powers and dominions lay their glory by.
Proud hearts and stubborn wills are put to flight,
the hungry fed, the humble lifted high.

Tell out, my soul, the glories of his word:
firm is his promise, and his mercy sure.
Tell out, my soul, the greatness of the Lord
to children's children and for evermore.

Timothy Dudley-Smith

Blest pair of Sirens, pledges of Heav'ns joy,
Sphear-born harmonious Sisters, Voice, and Vers,
Wed your divine sounds, and mixt power employ
Dead things with inbreath'd sense able to pierce,
And to our high-rais'd phantasie present,
That undisturbed Song of pure content,
Ay sung before the saphire-colour'd throne
To him that sits theron
With Saintly shout, and solemn Jubily,
Where the bright Seraphim in burning row
Their loud up-lifted Angel trumpets blow,
And the Cherubick host in thousand quires
Touch their immortal Harps of golden wires,
With those just Spirits that wear victorious Palms,
Hymns devout and holy Psalms
Singing everlastingly:
That we on Earth with undiscording voice
May rightly answer that melodious voice;
As once we did, till disproportion'd sin
Jarr'd against natures chime, and with harsh din
Broke the fair musick that all creatures made
To their great Lord, whose love their motion sway'd
In perfect Diapason, whilst they stood
In first obedience, and their state of good.
O may we soon again renew that Song,
And keep in tune with Heav'n, till God ere long
To his celestial consort us unite,
To live with him, and sing in endless morn of light.

John Milton

I bind unto myself today
The strong name of the Trinity
By invocation of the same
The Three in One, and One in Three.

I bind this day to me for ever,
By power of faith, Christ's incarnation.
His baptism in Jordan river;
His death on Cross for my salvation;
His bursting from the spiced tomb;
His riding up the heavenly way;
His coming at the day of doom;
I bind unto myself today.

I bind unto myself the power
Of the great love of Cherubim;
The sweet 'Well done' in judgment hour;
The service of the Seraphim,
Confessors' faith, Apostles' word,
The Patriarchs' prayers, the Prophets' scrolls,
All good deeds done unto the Lord,
And purity of virgin souls.

I bind unto myself today
The virtue of the starlit heaven,
The glorious sun's life-giving ray,
The whiteness of the moon at even,
The flashing of the lightning free,
The whirling wind's tempestuous shocks,
The stable earth, the deep salt sea,
Around the old eternal rocks.

I bind unto myself today
The power of God to hold and lead,
His eye to watch, his might to stay,
His ear to hearken to my need.
The wisdom of my God to teach,
His hand to guide, his shield to ward;
The word of God to give me speech,
His heavenly host to be my guard.

Against the demon snares of sin,
The vice that gives temptation force,
The natural lusts that war within,
The hostile men that mar my course;
Or few or many, far or nigh,
In every place, and in all hours,
Against their fierce hostility,
I bind to me these holy powers.

Against all Satan's spells and wiles,
Against false words of heresy,
Against the knowledge that defiles,
Against the heart's idolatry,
Against the wizard's evil craft,
Against the death-wound and the burning,
The choking wave, the poisoned shaft,
Protect me, Christ, till thy returning.

Christ be with me, Christ within me,
Christ behind me, Christ before me,
Christ beside me, Christ to win me,
Christ to comfort and restore me,
Christ beneath me, Christ above me,
Christ in quiet, Christ in danger,
Christ in hearts of all that love me,
Christ in mouth of friend and stranger.

I bind unto myself the name,
The strong name of the Trinity;
By invocation of the same,
The Three in One and One in Three.
Of whom all nature hath creation;
Eternal Father, Spirit, Word:
Praise to the Lord of my salvation,
Salvation is of Christ the Lord.

St Patrick's Breastplate,
translated Mrs C. F. Alexander

Father most holy, merciful and tender;
Jesus our Saviour, with the Father reigning;
Spirit all-kindly, Advocate, defender,
Light never waning;

Trinity sacred, Unity unshaken;
Deity perfect, giving and forgiving,
Light of the Angels, Life of the forsaken,
Hope of all living;

Maker of all things, all thy creatures praise thee;
Lo, all things serve thee through thy whole creation:
Hear us, Almighty, hear us as we raise thee
Heart's adoration.

To the all-ruling triune God be glory:
Highest and greatest, help thou our endeavour,
We too would praise thee, giving honour worthy,
Now and for ever.

Tenth-century office hymn

The world is charged with the grandeur of God.
It will flame out, like shining from shook foil;
It gathers to a greatness, like the ooze of oil
Crushed. Why do men then now not reck his rod?
Generations have trod, have trod, have trod;
And all is seared with trade; bleared, smeared with toil;
And wears man's smudge and shares man's smell: the soil
Is bare now, nor can foot feel, being shod.

And for all this, nature is never spent;
There lives the dearest freshness deep down things;
And though the last lights off the black West went
Oh, morning, at the brown brink eastwards, springs –
Because the Holy Ghost over the bent
World broods with warm breast and with ah! bright
    wings.

Gerard Manley Hopkins

All my hope on God is founded;
he doth still my trust renew.
Me through change and chance he guideth,
only good and only true.
God unknown,
He alone
Calls my heart to be his own.

Pride of man and earthly glory,
sword and crown betray his trust;
what with care and toil he buildeth,
tower and temple, fall to dust.
But God's power,
Hour by hour,
Is my temple and my tower.

God's great goodness aye endureth,
deep his wisdom, passing thought:
Splendour, light, and life attend him,
beauty springeth out of naught.
Evermore
From his store
New-born worlds rise and adore.

Daily doth th' Almighty Giver
bounteous gifts on us bestow;
His desire our soul delighteth,
pleasure leads us where we go.
Love doth stand,
At his hand;
Joy doth wait on his command.

Still from man to God eternal
sacrifice of praise be done,
High above all praises praising
for the gift of Christ his Son.
Christ doth call
One and all:
Ye who follow shall not fall.

Robert Bridges,
based on the German of J. Neander

O God of earth and altar,
Bow down and hear our cry,
Our earthly rulers falter,
Our people drift and die;
The walls of gold entomb us,
The words of scorn divide,
Take not thy thunder from us,
But take away our pride.

From all that terror teaches,
From lies of tongue and pen,
From all the easy speeches,
That comfort cruel men,
From sale and profanation
Of honour and the sword,
From sleep and from damnation,
Deliver us, good Lord!

Tie in a living tether,
The prince and priest and thrall,
Bind all our lives together,
Smite us and save us all;
In ire and exaltation
Aflame with faith, and free,
Lift up a living nation,
A single sword to thee.

G. K. Chesterton

Come, O thou Traveller unknown,
Whom still I hold, but cannot see,
My company before is gone,
And I am left alone with thee;
With thee all night I mean to stay,
And wrestle till the break of day.

I need not tell thee who I am,
My misery or sin declare;
Thyself hast called me by my name;
Look on thy hands, and read it there!
But who, I ask thee, who art thou?
Tell me thy name, and tell me now.

Yield to me now, for I am weak,
But confident in self-despair;
Speak to my heart, in blessings speak,
Be conquered by my instant prayer!
Speak, or thou never hence shalt move,
And tell me if thy name is Love.

'Tis Love! 'tis Love! Thou diedst for me!
I hear thy whisper in my heart!
The morning breaks, the shadows flee;
Pure universal Love thou art;
To me, to all, thy mercies move;
Thy nature and thy name is Love.

Charles Wesley

Eternal Ruler of the ceaseless round
of circling planets singing on their way;
Guide of the nations from the night profound
into the glory of the perfect day;
Rule in our hearts, that we may ever be
guided and strengthened and upheld by thee.

We are of thee, the children of thy love,
the brothers of thy well-beloved Son;
Descend, O Holy Spirit, like a dove,
into our hearts, that we may be as one;
As one with thee, to whom we ever tend;
As one with him, our Brother and our Friend.

We would be one in hatred of all wrong,
one in our love of all things sweet and fair,
One with the joy that breaketh into song,
one with the grief that trembles into prayer,
One in the power that makes thy children free
To follow truth, and thus to follow thee.

O clothe us with thy heavenly armour, Lord,
thy trusty shield, thy sword of love divine;
Our inspiration be thy constant word;
we ask no victories that are not thine:
Give or withhold, let pain or pleasure be;
Enough to know that we are serving thee.

J. W. Chadwick

He wants not friends that hath thy love,
And may converse and walk with thee,
And with thy Saints here and above,
With whom for ever I must be.

In the communion of Saints
In wisdom, safety and delight;
And when my heart declines and faints,
It's raisèd by their heat and light!

As for my friends, they are not lost;
The several vessels of thy fleet,
Though parted now, by tempests tost,
Shall safely in the haven meet.

Still we are centred all in thee,
Members, though distant, of one Head;
In the same family we be,
By the same faith and spirit led.

Before thy throne we daily meet
As joint petitioners to thee;
In spirit we each other greet,
And shall again each other see.

The heavenly hosts, world without end,
Shall be my company above;
And thou, my best and surest Friend,
Who shall divide me from thy love?

Richard Baxter

The Lord my pasture shall prepare,
And feed me with a shepherd's care;
His presence shall my wants supply,
And guard me with a watchful eye;
My noonday walks he shall attend,
And all my midnight hours defend.

When in the sultry glebe I faint,
Or on the thirsty mountain pant,
To fertile vales and dewy meads,
My weary wandering steps he leads,
Where peaceful rivers, soft and slow,
Amid the verdant landscape flow.

Though in a bare and rugged way
Through devious lonely wilds I stray
Thy bounty shall my pains beguile;
The barren wilderness shall smile
With sudden greens and herbage crowned,
And streams shall murmur all around.

Though in the paths of death I tread,
With gloomy horrors overspread,
My steadfast heart shall fear no ill,
For thou, O Lord, art with me still:
Thy friendly crook shall give me aid,
And guide me through the dreadful shade.

J. Addison

Hail, gladdening Light of his pure glory poured
Who is the immortal Father, heavenly, blest,
Holiest of Holies, Jesus Christ our Lord!
Now we are come to the sun's hour of rest,
The lights of evening round us shine.
We hymn the Father, Son, and Holy Spirit divine.

Worthiest art thou at all times to be sung
With undefiled tongue,
Son of our God, giver of life, alone:
Therefore in all the world thy glories, Lord, they own.

Third century, translated John Keble

Glory to thee, my God, this night
For all the blessings of the light;
Keep me, O keep me, King of kings,
Beneath thine own almighty wings.

Forgive me, Lord, for thy dear Son,
The ill that I this day have done,
That with the world, myself, and thee,
I, ere I sleep, at peace may be.

Teach me to live, that I may dread
The grave as little as my bed;
Teach me to die, that so I may
Rise glorious at the awful day.

O may my soul on thee repose,
And with sweet sleep mine eyelids close,
Sleep that may me more vigorous make,
To serve my God when I awake.

When in the night I sleepless lie,
My soul with heavenly thoughts supply;
Let no ill dreams disturb my rest,
No powers of darkness me molest.

You, my blest guardian, whilst I sleep
Close to my bed your vigils keep;
Divine love into me instill,
Stop all the avenues of ill.

Praise God, from whom all blessings flow,
Praise him, all creatures here below,
Praise him above, ye heavenly host,
Praise Father, Son, and Holy Ghost.

Bishop Thomas Ken

Now thank we all our God,
With heart and hands and voices,
Who wondrous things hath done,
In whom his world rejoices;
Who from our mother's arms
Hath blessed us on our way
With countless gifts of love,
And still is ours today.

O may this bounteous God
Through all our life be near us,
With ever joyful hearts
And blessed peace to cheer us;
And keep us in his grace,
And guide us when perplexed,
And free us from all ills
In this world and the next.

All praise and thanks to God
The Father now be given,
The Son, and him who reigns
With them in highest heaven,
The One eternal God,
Whom earth and heaven adore;
For thus it was, is now,
And shall be evermore.

M. Rinkart, translated C. Winkworth

Be thou my vision, O Lord of my heart,
Be all else but naught to me, save that thou art;
Be thou my best thought in the day and the night,
Both waking and sleeping, thy presence my light.

Be thou my wisdom, be thou my true word,
Be thou ever with me, and I with thee, Lord;
Be thou my great Father, and I thy true son;
Be thou in me dwelling, and I with thee one.

Be thou my breastplate, my sword for the fight;
Be thou my whole armour, be thou my true might;
Be thou my soul's shelter, be thou my strong tower:
O raise thou me heavenward, great Power of my power.

Riches I heed not, nor man's empty praise:
Be thou mine inheritance now and always;
Be thou and thou only the first in my heart:
O Sovereign of heaven, my treasure thou art.

High King of heaven, thou heaven's bright Sun,
O grant me its joys after vict'ry is won;
Great Heart of my own heart, whatever befall,
Still be thou my vision, O Ruler of all.

Eighth-century Irish
Translated Mary Byrne, versified Eleanor Hull

My soul, there is a country
Far beyond the stars,
Where stands a winged sentry
All skilful in the wars:

There above noise, and danger,
Sweet peace sits crowned with smiles,
And One born in a manger,
Commands the beauteous files.

He is thy gracious Friend,
And – O my soul, awake! –
Did in pure love descend,
To die here for thy sake.

If thou canst get but thither,
There grows the flower of peace,
The Rose that cannot wither,
Thy fortress and thy ease.

Leave then thy foolish ranges,
For none can thee secure
But one who never changes,
Thy God, thy life, thy cure.

Henry Vaughan

Benedictions

The benediction has perhaps always been the most moving of all prayers, associated as it is with the expression of deepest love, with parting, and with death. Sometimes blessings are pronounced authoritatively in the name of God, by a priest or minister, in which case they are put in the second person; at other times they are expressed in the form of a petition, in which case they are expressed in the first person. Some of the blessings quoted here are found in both forms. Many of them are adaptations of biblical words; the last two are by Bishop Ken and Cardinal Newman respectively.

Unto God's gracious mercy and protection we commit you.
The Lord bless you and keep you.
The Lord make his face to shine upon you and be gracious
   unto you.
The Lord lift up his countenance upon you, and give you
   peace, both now and for evermore.

Now unto him that is able to do exceeding abundantly
above all that we ask or think, according to the power that
worketh in us, unto him be the glory in the church and in
Christ Jesus throughout all ages, world without end.

Now the God of hope fill us with all joy and peace in
believing, that we may abound in hope, through the power
of the Holy Spirit; through Jesus Christ our Lord.

Now unto the King eternal, immortal, invisible, the only wise God, be honour and glory for ever and ever.

May the God of all grace, who hath called us into his eternal glory by Christ Jesus, make us perfect, stablish, strengthen, settle us; to whom be glory and dominion for ever and ever.

Now unto him that is able to keep us from falling, and to present us faultless before the presence of his glory, with exceeding joy, to the only wise God, our saviour, be glory and majesty, dominion and power, both now and for ever.

Now the God of peace, that brought again from the dead our Lord Jesus Christ, that great shepherd of the sheep, make you perfect in every good work to do his will, working in you that which is well-pleasing in his sight, through Jesus Christ: to whom be glory for ever and ever.

The peace of God, which passeth all understanding, keep your hearts and minds in the knowledge and love of God, and of his Son Jesus Christ, and the blessing of God Almighty, Father, Son, and Holy Ghost, be upon you and remain with you always.

To God the Father, who first loved us, and made us accepted in the Beloved; to God the son, who loved us, and washed us from our sins in his own blood; to God the Holy Ghost, who sheddeth the love of God abroad in our hearts: to the one true God be all love and all glory for time and eternity.

Go forth upon thy journey, Christian soul!
Go from this world! Go, in the Name of God
The Omnipotent Father, who created thee!
Go, in the Name of Jesus Christ, our Lord,
Son of the living God, Who bled for thee!
Go, in the Name of the Holy Spirit,
Who hath been poured out on thee! Go, in the name
Of Angels and Archangels; in the name
Of Thrones and Dominations; in the name
Of Princedoms and of Powers; and in the name
Of Cherubim and Seraphim, go forth.
Go in the name of Patriarchs and Prophets;
And of Apostles and Evangelists,
Of Martyrs and Confessors, in the name
Of holy Monks and Hermits; in the name
Of holy Virgins; and all Saints of God,
Both men and women, go! Go on thy course!
And may thy dwelling be the Holy Mount
Of Sion – through the same, through Christ our Lord.

Visions

'Where there is no vision, the people perish', runs a famous verse from the Book of Proverbs, and certainly the longing for, the dream, the hope of a better world is an integral part of our human make-up. Psychologists have dismissed it as a regression, a longing for the past security of childhood, as a projection of our feelings on to a barren heaven. There is no proving that view wrong, but those to whom these visions speak deeply will prefer to see them as an expression of the ultimate reality: that God is love, that being is gracious, that the ultimate ending of all humanity, despite everything, will be one of joy and glory.

But in the last days it shall come to pass,
that the mountain of the house of the Lord
shall be established in the top of the mountains,
and it shall be exalted above the hills;
and people shall flow unto it.
And many nations shall come, and say,
Come, and let us go up to the mountain of the Lord,
and to the house of the God of Jacob;
and he will teach us of his ways,
and we will walk in his paths:
for the law shall go forth of Zion,
and the word of the Lord from Jerusalem.
And he shall judge among many people,
and rebuke strong nations afar off,
and they shall beat their swords into ploughshares,
and their spears into pruninghooks;
nation shall not lift up a sword against nation;
neither shall they learn war any more.
But they shall sit every man under his vine and under his
    fig tree;
and none shall make them afraid;
for the mouth of the Lord of hosts hath spoken it.

Micah 4.1–4

Comfort ye, comfort ye my people,
saith your God.
Speak ye comfortably to Jerusalem,
and cry unto her,
that her warfare is accomplished,
that her iniquity is pardoned:
for she hath received of the Lord's hand
double for all her sins.

The voice of him that crieth in the wilderness,
Prepare ye the way of the Lord,
make straight in the desert a highway
for our God.
Every valley shall be exalted,
and every mountain and hill shall be made low;
and the crooked shall be made straight,
and the rough places plain:
And the glory of the Lord shall be revealed,
and all flesh shall see it together:
for the mouth of the Lord hath spoken it.

The voice said, Cry.
And he said, What shall I cry?
All flesh is grass,
and all the goodliness thereof is as the flower of the field.
The grass withereth, the flower fadeth:
but the word of our God shall stand for ever.

O Zion, that bringest good tidings,
get thee up into the high mountain:

O Jerusalem, that bringest good tidings,
lift up thy voice with strength;
lift it up, be not afraid;
say unto the cities of Judah,
Behold your God!
Behold, the Lord God will come with strong hand,
and his arm shall rule for him;
behold, his reward is with him,
and his work before him.
He shall feed his flock like a shepherd:
he shall gather the lambs with his arm,
and carry them in his bosom,
and shall gently lead those that are with young.

Isaiah 40.1–11

I am the good shepherd;
the good shepherd giveth his life for the sheep.
But he that is an hireling, and not the shepherd,
whose own the sheep are not,
seeth the wolf coming,
and leaveth the sheep, and fleeth:
and the wolf catcheth them,
and scattereth the sheep.
The hireling fleeth, because he is an hireling,
and careth not for the sheep.
I am the good shepherd,
and know my sheep, and am known of mine.
As the Father knoweth me, even so know I the Father;
and I lay down my life for the sheep.
And other sheep I have, which are not of this fold:
them also I must bring, and they shall hear my voice;
and there shall be one fold, and one shepherd.

John 10.11–16

What shall we then say to these things?
If God be for us, who can be against us?
He that spared not his own Son,
but delivered him up for us all,
how shall he not with him also freely give us all things?
Who shall lay any thing to the charge of God's elect?
It is God that justifieth. Who is he that condemneth?
It is Christ that died, yea rather, that is risen again,
who is even at the right hand of God,
who also maketh intercession for us.

Who shall separate us from the love of Christ?
Shall tribulation, or distress, or persecution, or famine,
or nakedness, or peril, or the sword?
As it written,
For thy sake we are killed all the day long;
we are accounted as sheep for the slaughter.
Nay, in all these things we are more than conquerors
through him that loved us.
For I am persuaded, that neither death, nor life,
nor angels, nor principalities, nor powers,
nor things present, nor things to come,
nor height, nor depth, nor any other creature,
shall be able to separate us from the love of God,
which is in Christ Jesus our Lord.

Romans 8.31–39

Though I speak with the tongues of men and of angels,
and have not charity,
I am become as sounding brass, or a tinkling cymbal.
And though I have the gift of prophecy,
and understand all mysteries, and all knowledge;
and though I have faith, so that I could remove mountains,
and have not charity,
I am nothing.
And though I bestow all my goods to feed the poor,
and though I give my body to be burned,
and have not charity,
it profiteth me nothing.

Charity suffereth long, and is kind;
charity envieth not;
charity vaunteth not itself, is not puffed up.
Doth not behave itself unseemly, seeketh not her own,
is not easily provoked, thinketh no evil;
Rejoiceth not in iniquity, but rejoiceth in the truth;
Beareth all things, believeth all things,
hopeth all things, endureth all things.
Charity never faileth:
but whether there be prophecies, they shall fail;
whether there be tongues, they shall cease;
whether there be knowledge, it shall vanish away.

For we know in part, and we prophesy in part.
But when that which is perfect is come,
then that which is in part shall be done away.

When I was a child, I spake as a child,
I understood as a child, I thought as a child:
but when I became a man, I put away childish things.

For now we see through a glass, darkly;
but then face to face:
now I know in part;
but then shall I know even as also I am known.

And now abideth faith, hope, charity, these three;
but the greatest of these is charity.

I Corinthians 13

And I saw a new heaven and a new earth;
for the first heaven and the first earth were passed away:
and there was no more sea.
And I John saw the holy city, new Jerusalem,
coming down from God out of heaven,
prepared as a bride adorned for her husband.
And I heard a great voice out of heaven saying,
Behold the tabernacle of God is with men,
and he will dwell with them,
and they shall be his people,
and God himself shall be with them,
and be their God.
And God shall wipe away all tears from their eyes;
and there shall be no more death,
neither sorrow, nor crying,
neither shall there be any more pain:
for the former things are passed away.
And he that sat upon the throne said,
Behold, I make all things new.
And he said unto me,
Write: for these words are true and faithful.

Revelation 21.1–5

There we shall rest and we shall see.
We shall see and we shall love.
We shall love and we shall praise.
Behold what shall be in the end
and shall not end.

St Augustine

Also in this He shewed me a little thing, the quantity of an hazel-nut, in the palm of my hand; and it was as round as a ball. I looked thereupon with eye of my understanding, and thought, 'What may this be?' And it was answered generally thus: 'It is all that is made.' I marvelled how it might last, for methought it might suddenly have fallen to naught for littleness. And I was answered in my understanding: 'It lasteth, and ever shall, for that God loveth it.' And so All-thing hath the Being by the love of God.

In this Little Thing I saw three properties. The first is that God made it; the second is that God loveth it, the third, that God keepeth it. But what is to me verily the Maker, Keeper, and the Lover – I cannot tell; for till I am substantially oned to Him, I may never have full rest or very bliss; that is to say, till I be so fastened to Him, that there is right nought that is made betwixt my God and me.

It needeth us to have knowing of the littleness of creatures and to hold as nought all-thing that is made, for to love and have God that is unmade. For this is the cause why we be not all in ease of heart or soul; that we seek here rest in those things that are so little, wherein is no rest, and know not our God that is All-mighty, All-wise, All-good. For He is the very rest. God willeth to be known, and it pleaseth Him that we rest in Him; for all that is beneath Him sufficeth not us. And this is the cause why that no soul is rested till it is made nought as to all things that are made. When it is willingly made nought, for love, to have Him that is all, then it is able to receive spiritual rest.

After this the Lord brought to my mind the longing that I had to Him afore. And I saw that nothing letted me but sin. And so I looked, generally, upon us all, and methought, 'If sin had not been, we should all have been clean and like to our Lord, as He made us.'

And thus, in my folly, afore this time often I wondered why by the great foreseeing wisdom of God the beginning of sin was not letted; for then, methought, all should have been well. This stirring was much to be forsaken, but nevertheless mourning and sorrow I made therefor, without reason and discretion.

But Jesus, who in this vision informed me of all that is needful in me, answered by this word and said, 'It behoved that there should be sin; but all shall be well, and all shall be well, and all manner of thing shall be well.'

Julian of Norwich

This River has been a terror to many, yea, the thoughts of it also have often frighted me; but now methinks I stand easy, my foot is fixed upon that upon which the feet of the Priests that bare the Ark of the Covenant stood, while Israel went over this Jordan. The waters indeed are to the palate bitter, and to the stomach cold; yet the thoughts of what I am going to, and of the conduct that waits for me on the other side, doth lie as a glowing coal at my heart.

I see myself now at the end of my Journey; my toilsome days are ended. I am going now to see that Head that was crowned with thorns, and that Face that was spit upon for me.

I have formerly lived by hear-say and Faith; but now I go where I shall live by Sight, and shall be with him in whose company I delight myself.

I have loved to hear my Lord spoken of and where-ever I have seen the print of his shoe in the earth, there I have coveted to set my foot too.

His Name has been to me as a civet-box; yea, sweeter than all perfumes. His Voice to me has been most sweet; and his Countenance I have more desired than they that have most desired the light of the Sun. His Word I did use to gather for my food, and for antidotes against my faintings. He has held me, and I have kept me from mine iniquities; yea, my steps hath he strengthened on his Way.

John Bunyan

Ring out ye Crystall sphears,
Once bless our human ears,
   (If ye have power to touch our senses so)
And let your silver chime
Move in melodious time;
   And let the Base of Heaven's deep Organ blow
And with your ninefold harmony
Make up full consort to th'Angelike symphony.

For if such holy Song
Enwrap our fancy long,
   Time will run back, and fetch the age of gold,
And speckl'd vanity
Will sicken soon and die,
   And leprous sin will melt from earthly mould,
And Hell it self will pass away,
And leave her dolorous mansions to the peering day.

Yea Truth, and Justice then
Will down return to men,
   Th'enameld Arras of the Rain-bow wearing,
And mercy set between
Thron'd in Celestiall sheen,
   With radiant feet the tissued clouds down stearing,
And Heav'n as at som festivall,
Will open wide the Gates of her high Palace Hall.

John Milton

I have a dream that one day every valley shall be exalted, every hill and mountain shall be made low. The rough places will be made plain, and the crooked places be made straight. With this faith we will be able to hew out of the mountains of despair the stone of hope. With this faith we will be able to work together, to pray together, to struggle together, to go to jail together, to stand up for freedom together, knowing we will be free one day.

This will be the day when all of God's children will be able to sing with new meaning, 'Let freedom ring'. So let freedom ring from the prodigious hilltops of New Hampshire; let freedom ring from the mighty mountains of New York. But not only that. Let freedom ring from Stone Mountain of Georgia. Let freedom ring from every hill and molehill of Mississippi, from every mountainside.

When we allow freedom to ring from every town and every hamlet, from every state and every city, we will be able to speed up that day when all of God's children, black men and white men, Jews and Gentiles, Protestants and Catholics, will be able to join hands and sing in the words of the old Negro spiritual, 'Free at last! Free at last! Great God Almighty, we are free at last!'

Martin Luther King

We shall not cease from exploration
And the end of all our exploring
Will be to arrive where we started
And know the place for the first time.
Through the unknown, remembered gate
Where the last of earth left to discover
Is that which was the beginning;
At the source of the longest river
The voice of the hidden waterfall
And the children in the apple-tree
Not known, because not looked for
But heard, half-heard, in the stillness
Between two waves of the sea.
Quick now, here, now, always –
A condition of complete simplicity
(Costing not less than everything)
And all shall be well and
All manner of thing shall be well
When the tongues of flame are in-folded
Into the crowned knot of fire
And the fire and the rose are one.

T. S. Eliot

ACKNOWLEDGMENTS

I am grateful to the following for permission to include copyright material:

The Right Revd Timothy Dudley-Smith and the Hope Publishing Company, Illinois, for 'Tell out, my soul, the greatness of the Lord'; Faber and Faber Ltd and Harcourt Brace Jovanovich for the concluding lines from 'East Coker' from T. S. Eliot's *Four Quartets*; The General Synod of the Church of England for the prayer beginning 'Father of all, we give you thanks and praise' from *The Alternative Service Book 1980, The Order for Holy Communion Rite A*. Martin Luther King's vision beginning 'I have a dream' comes from his speech delivered during the March on Washington on 28 August 1963, but I have not been able to trace the copyright holder. If I have unwittingly infringed any copyright, in this or any other case, I beg the owner's pardon.

INDEX OF OPENING WORDS